God's Care Is Everywhere

by Bruce Wannamaker
illustrated by
Helen Endres

Published by The Dandelion House
A Division of The Child's World

for distribution by VICTOR BOOKS™
A Division of Scripture Press Publications Inc.

Distributed by Scripture Press Publications, Wheaton, Illinois 60187.

Library of Congress Cataloging in Publication Data

Wannamaker, Bruce.
  God's care is everywhere.

  Summary: Affirms the evidences of God's love and
care in nature and in human relationships.
  1. Providence and government of God—Juvenile
literature.   [1. God.   2. Christian life]   I. Endres,
Helen, ill.   II. Title.
BT135.M56   231'.5   82-7244
ISBN 0-89693-202-8   AACR2

Published by The Dandelion House, A Division of The Child's World, Inc.
© 1982 SP Publications, Inc. All rights reserved. Printed in U.S.A.

3 4 5 6 7 8 9 10 11 12 R 89 88 87 86

God's
Care
Is
Everywhere

y ou cannot see. . .

the wind. . .

but you know it is there!

You can feel it blowing your hair. . .
pulling your kite into the sky!

You can watch trees bending
as it blows by.

You cannot see the wind,
but you know it is there.

You cannot see God. . .

but you know He is there.

You can feel God's love and care through those who love Him.

You can feel God's love and care when Mother holds you close.

You can feel God's love and care
when you have fallen. . .
    and Dad picks you up.

You can feel God's love and care
when you are afraid. . .

. . .and Grandma takes your hand.

TOYS

You cannot see God,
but you know He is there.
You can feel God's love and care
through those who love Him.

You cannot see God,
but you know He is there.
You can see the world God made.

Pick a flower,
and you will see God's care. . .
for God sends the sunshine and the rain
to help the flowers grow.

Watch the birds
in a cherry tree. . .

or a squirrel
with an acorn. . .

or a chipmunk
with a seed.

If God so cares for His animals,
think how much more God cares
for you.

God cares for you wherever you are. . .

at home alone. . .

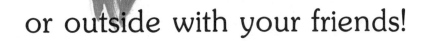

or outside with your friends!

God cares for you
at all times. . .

when you are sad. . .

. . .and when you are happy. . .

when you are sick. . .

. . .and when you are well again!

God cares for you through every day. . .

. . . .and every night.

God cares for you
wherever you are,
for God's care is
everywhere!